The Wonder of
WOLVES

Adapted from Tom Wolpert's *Wolf Magic for Kids*
by Patricia Lantier-Sampon

D1505826

Gareth Stevens Publishing
MILWAUKEE

For a free color catalog describing Gareth Stevens' list of high-quality books, call 1-800-341-3569 (USA) or 1-800-461-9120 (Canada).

Library of Congress Cataloging-in-Publication Data

Lantier-Sampon, Patricia.
   The wonder of wolves / adapted from Tom Wolpert's Wolf magic for kids by Patricia Lantier-Sampon ;
photography by Bob Baldwin, Daniel J. Cox, and Lynn Rogers.
      p.   cm. — (Animal wonders)
   Includes index.
   Summary: Text and photographs introduce that misunderstood creature of northern habitats, the wolf.
   ISBN 0-8368-0859-2
   1. Wolves—Juvenile literature. [1. Wolves.] I. Baldwin, Bob, ill. II. Cox, Daniel J., 1960- ill. III. Rogers,
Lynn L., ill. IV. Wolpert, Tom. Wolf magic for kids. V. Title. VI. Series.
   QL737.C22L264   1992
   599.74'442—dc20   92-16948

North American edition first published in 1992 by
Gareth Stevens Publishing
1555 North RiverCenter Drive, Suite 201
Milwaukee, WI 53212, USA

This U.S. edition is abridged from *Wolf Magic for Kids*, copyright © 1990 by NorthWord Press, Inc., and
written by Tom Wolpert, first published in 1990 by NorthWord Press, Inc., and published in a library
edition by Gareth Stevens, Inc. Additional end matter copyright © 1992 by Gareth Stevens, Inc.

Cover design: Kristi Ludwig

Printed in the United States of America

   2 3 4 5 6 7 8 9 98 97 96 95 94 93

Some people think wolves are fierce animals, but this is not really true. In fact, the wolf is the *ancestor* of our oldest animal friend, the dog.

The gray wolf lives in North America. It looks a little like a German shepherd, but it is larger and shaggier.

Wolves can be many colors, although most are gray. Some are black, golden brown, rusty red, or even pure white.

The timber wolf lives among the trees in wooded areas of North America. Its forest home is dark and shadowy.

The dark coat of the timber wolf helps it hide from its forest enemies.

Tundra wolves have pure, white fur. They live in cold, snowy areas.

Their thick, white fur keeps them warm and helps them hide in the snow.

Wolves *mate* in late winter. The mother digs a special *den* for her babies before they are born. This den must be in a dry spot close to a river or stream so there will be plenty of water nearby.

New baby wolves are called pups. The whole wolf family stays near the den to protect the mother and her pups. This family is called a pack, and the members travel and hunt together.

Baby wolves cannot see or hear when they are born.

At first, they do nothing but eat and sleep all day.

The pups now belong to the wolf family, or pack. The leader is usually a male wolf. All the wolves in the pack obey the leader.

When the pack makes a kill, the leader eats first. Then the other wolves can have a turn at the meat.

When the wolves have finished eating, they usually take a nap in a spot the leader chooses.

Each pack also has a
female leader. She helps
control the other wolves.

Wolf packs can be large. But there is still only one male and female leader.

Wolf pups can see and hear very well by the time they are three weeks old. Now they can go outside and explore the world for the first time.

All the wolves in the pack take turns watching the new pups while the mother hunts for food. She carries food for her babies inside her stomach until she gets back to the den.

The pups begin to sleep outside when they are about three months old. Now it is time to live with the rest of the pack.

Wolves are great hunters. They search their *territories* for *prey*.

Wolves often travel for many miles to find food.

Wolves are also strong runners. They travel far and wide while hunting, and they can trot as far as forty miles without stopping to rest.

Wolves hunt for food by using their *keen* sense of smell. The pack often circles its prey, sometimes after *tracking* it for a long time. This is how the pack works together to find and catch its food.

After eating, the wolves rest in the sun for a few hours. Then they return to finish their food and chew on the bones that remain.

Wolves can make many different sounds. These sounds help them "speak" to each other. Each sound has a special meaning that other wolves can easily understand. If a wolf is excited, it whimpers. If it senses danger, it makes a "wuff" sound.

We don't know for sure why wolves howl.

They might howl to tell other packs to keep away.

Wolves are exciting and beautiful animals that have survived side by side with their prey for thousands of years.

These wolves are an important part of our natural world.

Glossary

ancestor — a relative from long ago

den — a home or shelter

keen — sharp or sensitive

mate — to join together (animals) to produce young

prey — an animal hunted or caught for food

territory — a certain area of land, or a region

tracking — following the trail of a person or animal

Index